EASY JAZZ FAVORITES
15 Selections For Young Jazz Ensembles

Contents

AIN'T MISBEHAVIN'

Bass

Words by ANDY RAZAF
Music by THOMAS WALLER and HARRY BROOKS
Arranged by BOB LOWDEN

ALL THE THINGS YOU ARE
(From VERY WARM FOR MAY)

Lyrics by OSCAR HAMMERSTEIN II
Music by JEROME KERN
Arranged by MICHAEL SWEENEY

BASS

BLUE TRAIN
(Blue Trane)

Bass

By JOHN COLTRANE
Arranged by MICHAEL SWEENEY

BASS

CARAVAN
(From SOPHISTICATED LADIES)

Words and Music by DUKE ELLINGTON,
IRVING MILLS and JUAN TIZOL
Arranged by MICHAEL SWEENEY

BASS

CHAMELEON

Bass

By HERBIE HANCOCK, PAUL JACKSON,
HARVEY MASON and BENNIE MAUPIN
Arranged by MICHAEL SWEENEY

BASS

FLY ME TO THE MOON
(In Other Words)

Words and Music by BART HOWARD
Arranged by JERRY NOWAK

BASS

BASS

THE GIRL FROM IPANEMA
(Garôta De Ipanema)

Original Words by VINICIUS DE MORAES
Music by ANTONIO CARLOS JOBIM
Arranged by JOHN BERRY

BASS

IN THE MOOD

By JOE GARLAND
Arranged by MICHAEL SWEENEY

Bass

BASS

INSIDE OUT

BASS

By MICHAEL SWEENEY

BASS

MILESTONES

By MILES DAVIS
Arranged by PETER BLAIR

A NIGHTINGALE SANG
IN BERKELEY SQUARE

Lyric by ERIC MASCHWITZ
Music by MANNING SHERWIN
Arranged by ROGER HOLMES

Bass

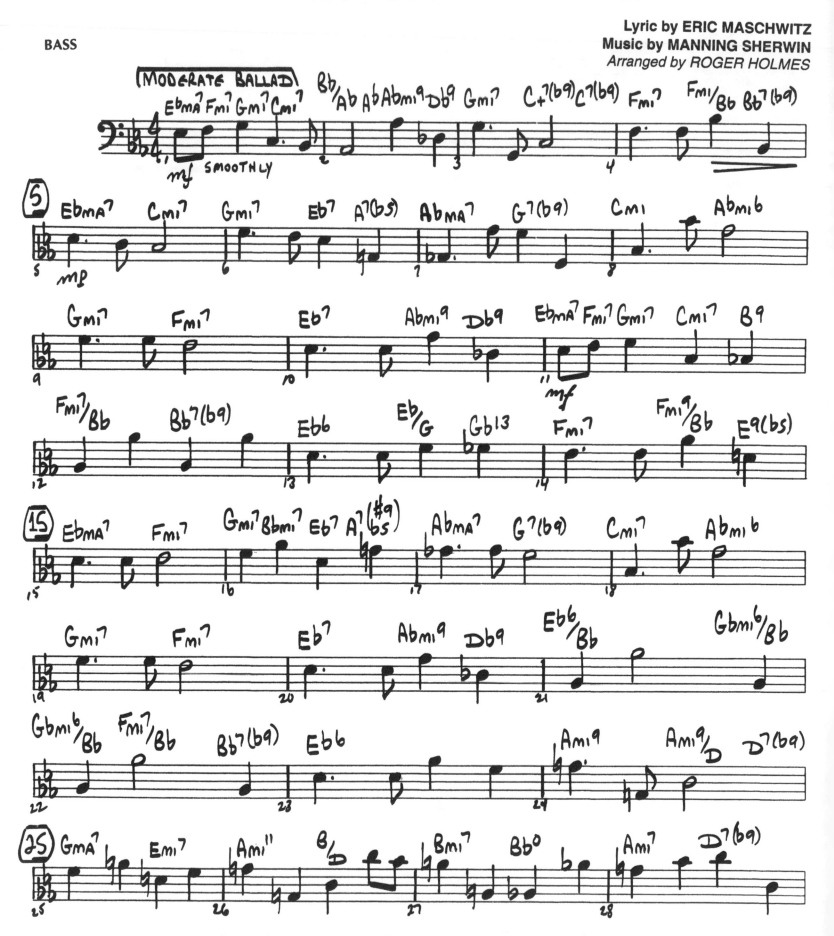

BASS

GRAD. DECRESC.   Ritard

ONE NOTE SAMBA
(Samba De Uma Nota So)

Original Lyrics by NEWTON MENDONCA
English Lyrics by ANTONIO CARLOS JOBIM
Music by ANTONIO CARLOS JOBIM
Arranged by JERRY NOWAK

BASS

MCA music publishing

BASS

ROUTE 66

BASS

By BOBBY TROUP
Arranged by MICHAEL SWEENEY

BASS

ST. LOUIS BLUES

Words and Music by W.C. HANDY
Arranged by MICHAEL SWEENEY

BASS

BASS

WHEN I FALL IN LOVE

Words by EDWARD HEYMAN
Music by VICTOR YOUNG
Arranged by ROGER HOLMES

Bass